FROM THE WHEEL TO THE INTERNET!

CHILDREN'S TECHNOLOGY BOOKS

THE HISTORY OF COMPUTERS

CHILDREN'S COMPUTERS & TECHNOLOGY BOOKS

pfiffikus

EDUCATIONAL BOOKS FOR CHILDREN K-12

How amazing is that box?
Why is it called one of
the greatest inventions?

People nowadays have become used to computers. But have you ever asked yourself about the origin of computers? Kids, let us try to dig in more about computers.

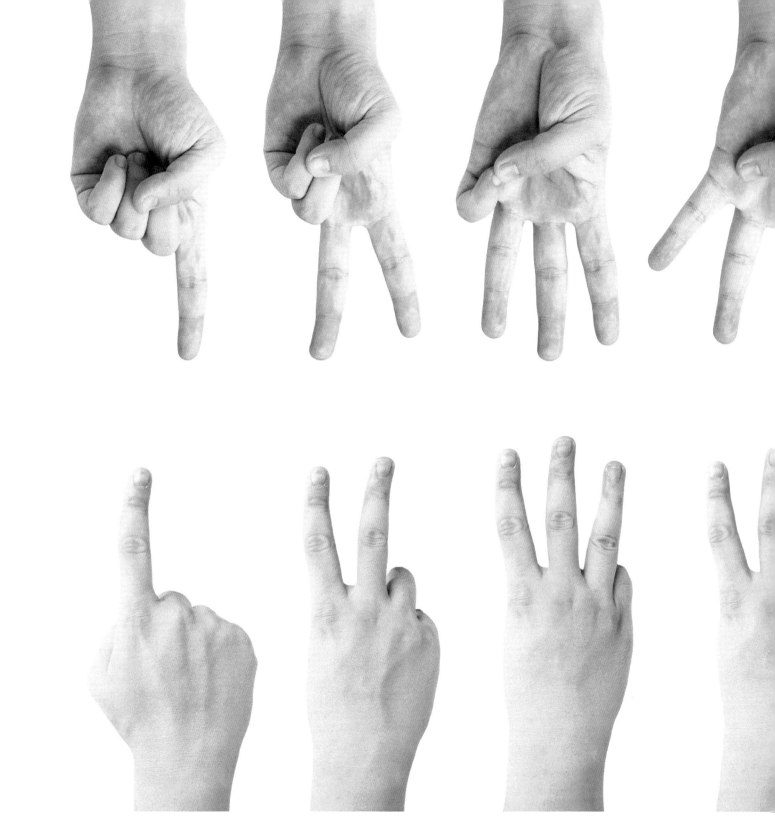

COUNTING TOOL

Did you know that the main purpose of computer has always been just to help us people to count?

Our ancestors used bones with notches carved into them in order to represent and manipulate numbers. Another form of manual counting was quipu, used by Inca Indians. Quipu is a knotted string which is somewhat similar to simple notched sticks.

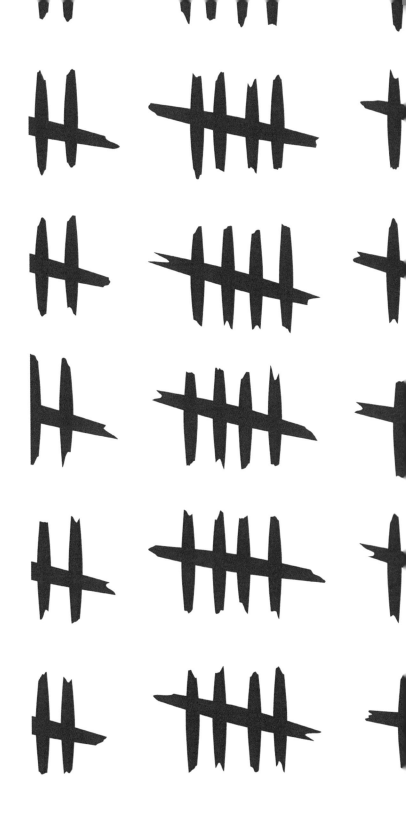

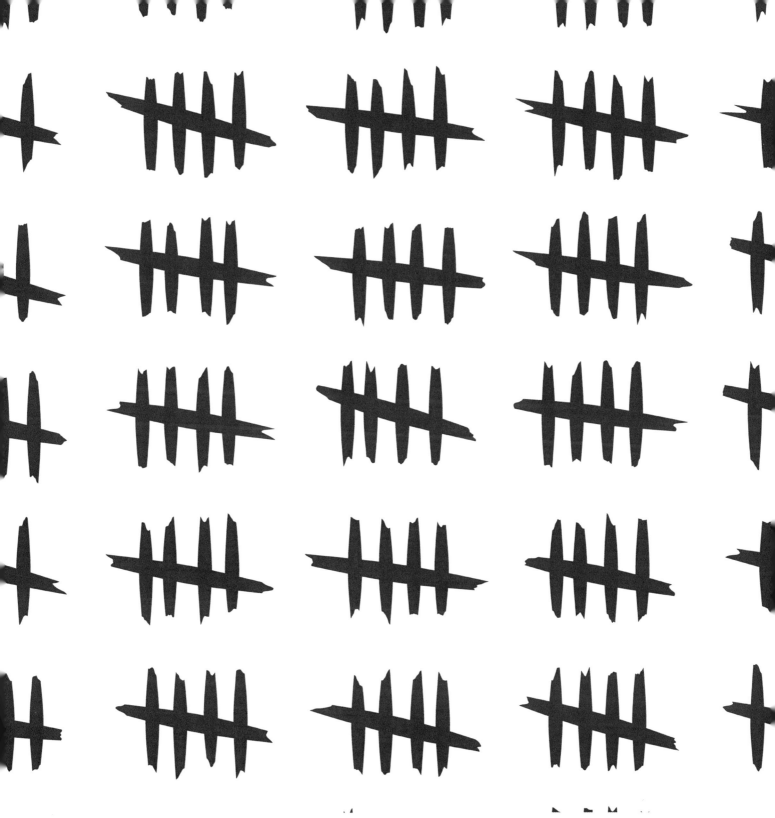

ABACUS

Approximately 4,000 years ago, Chinese people invented the first machine for counting and calculating, the abacus. An abacus is made of a wooden frame, wooden beads, and metal rods. Each bead on each rod has a specific value.

The beads at
the center of
the abacus
are used to
perform specific
operations
like addition,
subtraction,
multiplication
and division.

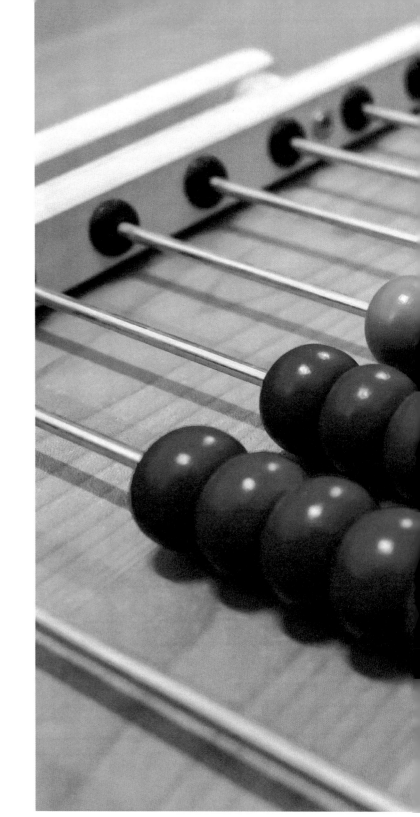

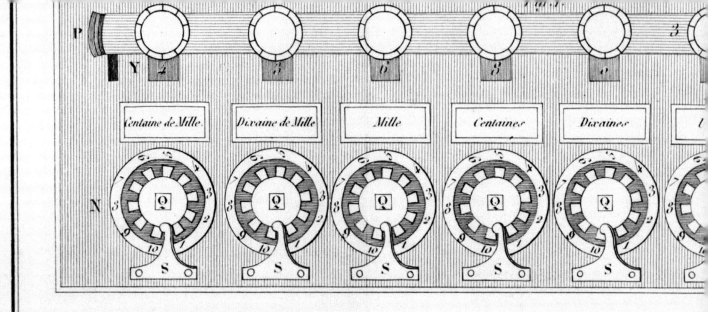

P

Y 4 3 6 8 0 3

Centaine de Mille. Dixaine de Mille. Mille. Centaines. Dixaines.

N

S S S S S

Fig. 2.

GEAR DRIVEN MACHINES

In 1642, A French mathematician named Blaise Pascal invented the first mechanical and automatic computer. Eventually he called this La Pascaline or Pascal's machine.

ELECTRO-MECHANICAL MACHINES

In 1890, 50 years after Charles Babbage's death, Norman Hollerith invented a tabulating machine. It is mainly used to speed up the work involved in the government census.

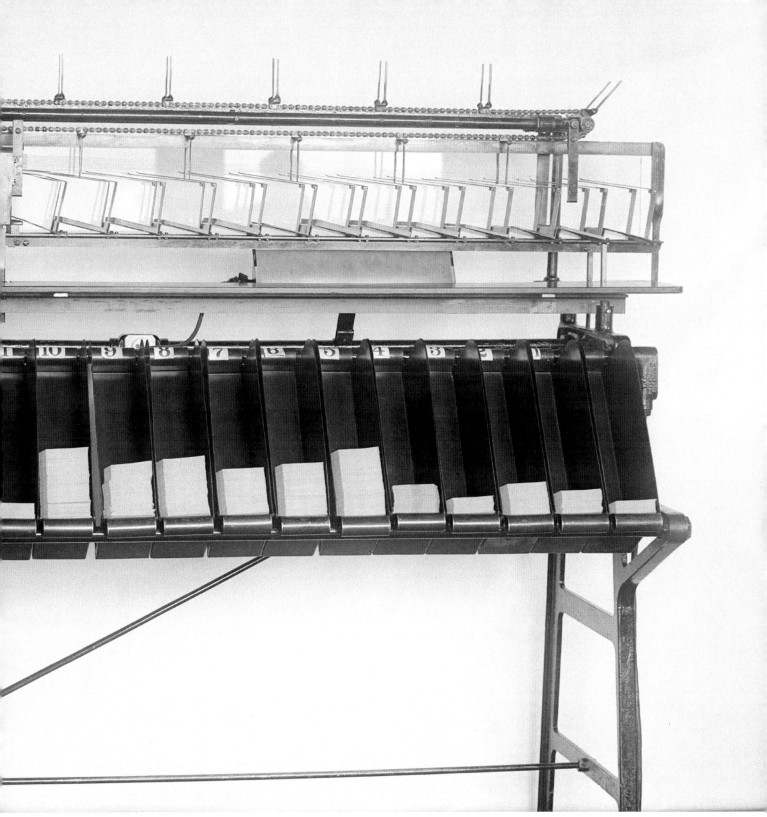

FIRST GENERATION

In 1946, the Electronic Numerical Integrator and Computer (ENIAC) was created by John William Mauchly and John Presper Eckert. It could do 5000 additions per second and 300 multiplications.

In 1951, the
proponents of
ENIAC introduced
another design
of this amazing
machine known as
the Universal
Automatic
Computer
(UNIVAC).

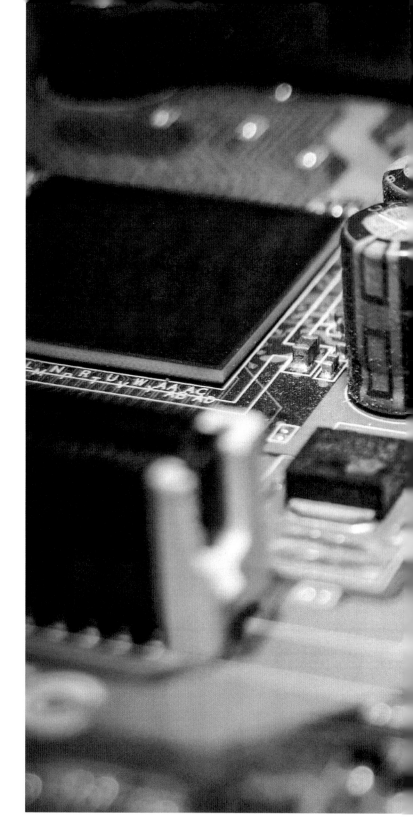

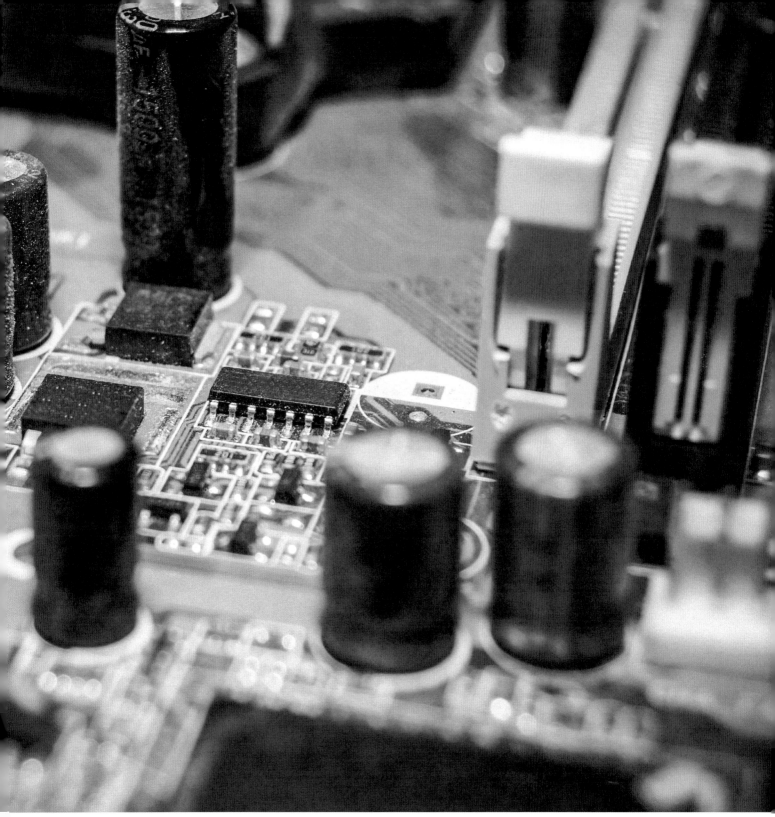

SECOND GENERATION

1956-1963 was called the Era of Transistor. Transistors were a huge advancement over vacuum tubes for transmitting information.

THIRD GENERATION

Transistors
were indeed
a tremendous
breakthrough
in computer
advancement,
yet no one
could predict
that thousands
of transistors
could still be
compacted into
small space.

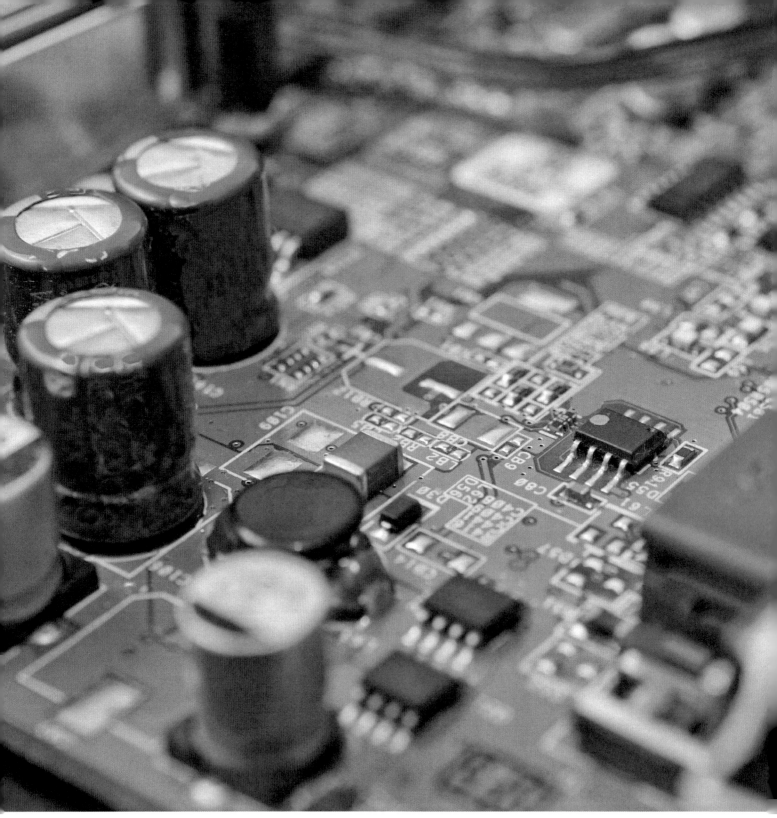

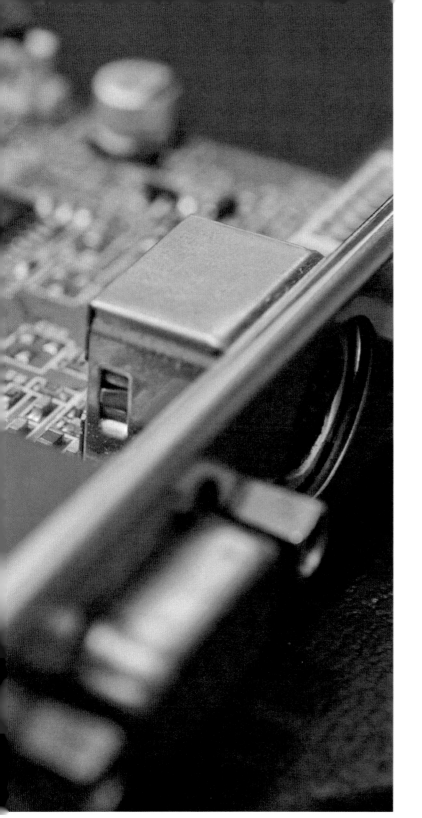

This is called
the integrated
circuit and
is sometimes
referred to as
the semiconductor
chip.

FOURTH GENERATION

Most electronic
devices today
use some form
of integrated
circuits. These
are placed
on printed
circuit boards
or the mother
board. Then the
invention of the
microprocessor
arises.

This amazing
single chip
is capable of
doing all the
processing of
a full-scale
computer.

MAINFRAMES TO PERSONAL COMPUTERS

In the early 1970s, personal computers started to invade human technological history. Today, almost every home has this very powerful machine.

Computers share information as they are linked together. Connecting computers over greater distances, known as wide area networks (WANs), can offer us greater benefits.

Today, people remain connected with one another anywhere in the globe through the use of the Internet. It is a global network of individual computers and LANs or Local Area Networks.

Computers are one of the amazing technological inventions that are continually being modified and upgraded for the benefit of youth and adults alike. In human history, the computer revolution is the fastest-growing technology.

Made in the USA
Las Vegas, NV
05 February 2021